MW00946357

The IT Book TWO

A Time for Living

A Time for Dying

Kathie Gedden

Dedication

To Bill Mercer, my husband and my friend,
who has given love, understanding, joy and
meaning to every moment for the past 22 years

To Bev, Joe, Mary, and Paul,
who inspired me to write another book

To my many friends, friends forever

Special thanks to my sister,
Mary Gedden Weaver,
my editor

Very special thanks to my dear friend,
Terry Stuart, who took care of everything
to do with publishing this book

Other Books by Kathie Gedden

Beginning Piano: The Way I Teach It
  (www.amazon.com)

The IT Book
  Short Stories of Encouragement for
  Children of All Ages
  (www.inspiringvoices.com)
  (www.amazon.com)

MY FATHER
  (www.amazon.com)

TABLE OF CONTENTS

POEMS FROM MY HEART

FLY IT

More than 35 years ago, I was completing a visit to Hawaii. When I was ready to fly back to Des Moines, Iowa, there was an airline strike. Under the circumstances, I found myself waiting on standby for a flight. I was originally scheduled to fly from Honolulu to San Francisco or Los Angeles and then on to Des Moines. Little did I know that I was about to embark on one of the adventures of my life.

I finally boarded a plane in Honolulu, but it did not take me to California. Instead, it landed in Seattle, Washington, in the evening. I was told, along with a large number of other passengers, to report to the ticket counter the next morning for further instructions. I learned that the ticket counter opened at 4 am, so I prepared to join many of my fellow passengers for a few hours of attempted sleep on the floor of the Seattle airport.

Knowing I would have to be first in line to have a chance at a flight, I found a spot on the floor as close as possible to the ticket counter. Even though I was first in line at 4 am, I was told that it might be several days before I could get a flight. The look on my face must have prompted that ticket agent to have mercy on me. He said that if I would not tell anyone and if I was willing to be routed through Anchorage, Alaska, they would pay for me to go to a motel to sleep for a half day before the flight took off. I gratefully accepted.

1

Several hours later, I found myself on a plane to Anchorage. I had never been to Alaska. As we started descending over the Aleutian Range before approaching and landing at Anchorage, I was in awe at the scenery, the miles and miles of bright green evergreen trees.

Upon arriving at the Anchorage airport, we were told that in precisely four hours the plane would take off again, this time for Minneapolis, Minnesota. So I had four hours in Anchorage, Alaska. I was told that I could take the airport limousine, which turned out to be an old van, to downtown Anchorage. This I did. As I was walking along the streets of downtown Anchorage, the thought occurred to me that no one would believe that I had been there. So I proceeded to buy a few items for proof. I particularly remember an Alaskan cookbook that I purchased and kept for many years.

Then I had a memorable experience. I could see the Pacific Ocean at the end of the street. I walked down to the water just as the sun was setting over the ocean. It was an awesome moment when I realized that only a couple days previously I had seen that sun set over the Pacific Ocean in Hawaii.

Back at the airport, I boarded the plane for an overnight flight to Minneapolis. The next morning I boarded a much smaller plane for a shaky ride home to the Des Moines, Iowa, airport.

FLY IT

UNDERSTAND IT

When I was 28 years old, I met and married a man 14 years my senior. This man's first wife had died of cancer only six months before, after years of surgery and sickness. At that time I knew nothing about death or about grieving, and especially about the dangers of marrying so soon after a death. This man also had three children, a boy nine and two girls, ages 12 and 13, who had just lost their mother. I was embarking on one of the most painful experiences of my life.

Before the wedding everyone seemed happy and in favor of it. The children were even in the wedding. But after the wedding, reality set in. Of course, as in most things in life, it wasn't all bad. In fact, the little nine-year-old boy was one of the kindest souls I have ever met. In ten years he never said an unkind word to me. He even called me mom. He was like an angel to me. He got me through. He very much needed a mom.

He was having problems in school with the new math and other subjects. I went to his teachers and helped him through that year with his schoolwork.

The twelve-year-old girl was a bundle of energy. I could hardly keep up with her. Everything she did, she did in a hurry. But she was a lot of help too. She helped in the kitchen, and I helped her when she wanted to learn to sew (one of the skills I had focused on in the past few years). But when I started out to make a dress, it might take me a few weeks. When she did it, it had to be done in one day. For the most part she seemed happy, but there was one period of several months that she seemed very bitter about something.

The thirteen-year-old girl rarely ever had a happy moment. Everything seemed difficult for her. School was very hard for her. I went to her teachers and learned that her mother had been there many times trying to help her. Her mother had been a teacher. Once she screamed at her father in front of me for "getting a stepmother for me." When she and I were there alone, she would scream at me if I didn't fold an article of clothing the way her mother had folded it. Then she would go to her bed and cry and cry for a long, long time while I sat and tried to comfort her. This happened many times. Her mother had been her whole world, and her mother died.

I was young and sensitive. I took everything to heart. I took everything personally. I didn't understand how she, and sometimes her sister, could treat me so when I was trying so hard to help them.

I often went to their mother's grave at the cemetery. I took flowers. I sat and talked to their mother. I told her their problems and asked her to help me help them. I had learned from neighbors, relatives and friends and from the children's love for her, how very kind she was.

It was not until about 45 years later, just recently, that I began to understand. It happened while my husband, Bill, and I were watching the DVD "Sarah Plain and Tall".

Anna, the young daughter whose mother had died, was visiting at a neighbor's house. She said to the woman there: "You have nice things all around you." The woman said: "Your mama had nice things. Do you remember?" Anna said: "A little. I remember candlesticks on the table, a painting of a black bird, a quilt Mama made, stars of color. Papa put them away." The woman replied: "I know."

A woman named Sarah came from the east in response to an ad that Jacob, Anna's father, had put in the paper for a wife and someone to help with his two young children. During the night, Sarah was awakened by a loud, mournful sobbing. She hurried and found Anna crying: "Mama, Mama." Sarah held Anna in her arms. Through her tears, Anna said: "Maggie gave me this shawl Mama made for her. Papa put away all the things that she loved, a quilt, her picture. Papa doesn't understand."

Sarah went downstairs and found Jacob on the porch. She said to him: "Perhaps it is a mistake to deprive the children of their memories." In a loud voice, he told her no, and rode off on his horse.

While he was gone, Sarah took the mother's things out of a trunk, and placed them around the house. When Jacob came back, he saw what she had done, but he did not put them back.

All of this had a profound effect on me. I realized that in those ten years that I had been with that family, I had never seen a picture of that mother in that little house. Her name had never been mentioned. We had never talked about her. The children had never been to the cemetery.

I am a compassionate person and am still somewhat shocked that in the past 45 years, until I saw that movie, I had not been able to understand their anger toward me. This had generated a lot of anger and hurt in me also.

I had never tried so hard in all my life to help anyone as much as I did those three children, but there were some things I just did not understand.

Their anger was not really at me (though it certainly appeared to be), but it was their attempt to grieve the loss of their mother, intensified by being denied the opportunity to see her picture, to talk about her, to go to the cemetery, to be understood. I just happened to be the only safe outlet for their anger and hurt. I lasted in that painful marriage for ten years, until the girls were married and the son in college.

I can't help wondering if some of these things would also apply to children who are deprived of their parents, even part time, through divorce.

Perhaps we can in some way lessen the suffering in this world if we can

UNDERSTAND IT

TRANSLATE IT

In August of 1984, my cousin Josef and his son, Christoph, came from Germany to visit our father Joseph, our mother Katherine, and all of our family in Des Moines, Iowa. As I mentioned in the first IT Book, Josef and I had written to each other for 30 years before we met in person in 1984. My father, Joseph, was Josef's uncle. My dad came to the United States from Germany on an ocean liner in 1928 at age 18.

After the visit of Josef and Christoph, I devoted a year of my life to studying German. I wanted to be able to communicate in German with our relatives in Germany.

I studied German at a university in Oklahoma City. I was extremely fortunate to have Frau Schneider as my teacher. She was not only a superb teacher, but her German heritage made the opportunity to learn from her full of rich experiences. Enjoying words and languages as I do, and having a definite goal of being able to communicate with our loved ones in Germany, gave me all the motivation and inspiration I needed.

I reveled in the opportunity.

I thoroughly enjoyed that year, and while I am no expert in German, I have been able to read and write enough to communicate somewhat. I communicate by short letters and emails with some of my cousins in Germany who do not know any English. When we occasionally receive a letter or email in German, I am able to translate it into English for our family here in the United States.

Now my cousin, Josef, emails me in German, and I answer him in English. This gives both of us the opportunity to translate. I use my English/German dictionary to translate words in his letters that I do not know, and this gives me an opportunity to learn more German.

TRANSLATE IT

ACCOMPANY IT

During the four years that I was in high school, I accompanied the orchestra on the piano.

Memorizing music is not easy for me, but sight-reading is. To sight-read a piece of music means to play the music the first time you see it. I did a lot of sight-reading during those four years playing with the orchestra.

I went to a Catholic all girls high school taught by Catholic nuns. We had a large orchestra, and we played quite a varied repertoire of music. I very much enjoyed playing the piano with the orchestra. The sister in charge of the orchestra was also my piano teacher. She was a master musician and teacher. However, in those days, nuns were not allowed to conduct an orchestra in public. So when it came time for a concert for the public on the stage in the auditorium, an elderly professor from Drake University would come to direct the concert. His name was Professor Noyes. I still have to laugh at his name because it is pronounced the same as noise. He was very gruff, never smiled, and said very little. He always made me somewhat nervous.

As long as I live, I will never forget one of those concerts. I was seated at the piano ready to play what I thought was a very loud piece of music. I was watching him and was ready to loudly strike the first chord when he directed us to begin.

This I did. The only problem was that I was on the wrong piece. I came down with a loud chord on that first count while all the rest of the orchestra played the correct song. He glared at me and made the conducting motion for everyone to immediately stop playing. I then turned to the correct page, and we continued on with the concert. Even though I do not recall him, or my teacher, or any of my family who were in the audience, or anyone else ever mentioning my ghastly mistake, I will never forget it.

In spite of that one disaster, I still love to

ACCOMPANY IT

ADVENTURE IT

In the short story, ADVERTISE IT, in the first *IT Book*, I told one of the many adventures that my husband, Bill, and I had during the years that we lived in a little cottage near Evergreen Lake in Evergreen, Colorado.

This story is about more of our adventures there.

Denver, Colorado, the mile-high city, is exactly one mile or 5,280 feet above sea level. Evergreen is approximately 7,000 feet above sea level, varying in different areas of town. Evergreen is west of Denver up the mountain.

Evergreen usually gets a lot of snow, but in March of 2003 when we lived there, we got more than a lot of snow. Bill remembers hearing that we got 119 inches, just short of ten feet in two days!

We were without power for four days and four nights. Power lines iced over and snapped. We had no electricity, but we did have a small gas stove. We had to light it by hand with a match because the electric starters would not work.

We had no garage. Our two cars were totally buried in snow. Bill shoveled all of one day to uncover one of them. That night it snowed and buried that car again. Bill thinks he remembers uncovering both cars by the end of the second day. It was necessary that we get at least one of the cars uncovered so that we could get inside and turn on the heater to get warm.

As we remember it, on the fourth day, the road was plowed. Our road connected with a main road that went almost straight up. Bill got into his car after the road was plowed and attempted several times, unsuccessfully, to drive up that hill. He came back and got my car which had Blizzak snow tires on it, and drove up the hill without any problem. He then cautiously drove to a grocery store.

Evergreen Lake was a beautiful sight in the winter. When the ice was thick enough, a certain area of the lake was plowed and the ice smoothed for ice skating. There were floodlights along the edge of the lake above the skating area, allowing for nighttime skating. On New Year's Eve, skating was allowed until almost midnight at which time there was a marvelous fireworks display. We could see this from our little cottage.

Bill recalls one night when he drove into our parking area next to the cottage. Just as he was about to open his car door to get out, he heard a noise. The next thing he knew, 19 elk stampeded down the hill, across the road and between our two cars as he sat in the car and counted them. When we lived for a time in Estes Park, we sometimes counted from 50 to 100 elk in our big yard at one time.

When we first moved to Evergreen, Bill said he was going to grow tomatoes. I warned him that I had heard that the elk and deer eat every growing thing. However, he proceeded with his plan. He took the best care of those tomato plants.

They grew beautifully. One evening he said that they would be perfect the following day. Alas! The elk also knew when they were ready for picking, and they enjoyed their feast just before Bill went out to collect his harvest.

There was a small house on a hill just across the road from our cottage. This house had a front deck seven and a half or eight feet high. The young woman who lived there put a beautiful pot of geraniums on her high deck, relieved that there was at least one outdoor place free from elk.

But when she came home, she found that much of her beautiful plant had been eaten!

The next day Bill saw a cow elk climb the steps to her deck, feast on the flowers, and then walk back down.

Bill told me this elk story. He had three friends who were going elk hunting in a National Forest near Evergreen. They drove up and parked their cars in the designated parking area. Across the road was a game sanctuary where hunting was prohibited. After they got out of their cars, they glanced across the road and saw a herd of elk along the fence looking at them.

The men turned and walked in the National Forest where, in a whole day of hunting, they never saw a single elk!

Evergreen Lake was beautiful in the summertime, too. There was a path all the way around the lake. It was a lovely place to walk. One day I watched an elk swim all the way across the lake. Birdwatchers loved it there. When we lived there, I saw a poster with the names of different birds. The birdwatchers would keep tally of how many of each kind of bird they saw each day. There were ducks and beavers, too. There were paddle boats that people could rent to paddle around the lake. Thankfully, no motor boats were allowed. Up on a hill to the south of the lake (just west of our little cottage) was a lush green golf course.

On the west side of the lake was a beautiful, modern lake house where weddings were often held. Just to the west of that was a lovely park with picnic tables and awesome views of mountains.

These are a few of the many adventures that we had in Evergreen. There are so many ways to

ADVENTURE IT

HIKE IT

One of my favorite hikes was along the eastern edge of Shadow Mountain Lake, just south of Grand Lake in Colorado's Rocky Mountain National Park. It always renewed my spirit. It was peaceful. It was quiet.

We usually parked in a small parking area at the north end of the trail, then hiked south, and then back up north again to the car. When we went all the way, it could take a whole afternoon.

Although the campground at the southern end of the trail was often packed with people, we rarely met anyone along that long trail. We often stopped to look at the lovely lake on the western side of the trail, to hear the water lapping on the shore, to enjoy the wildflowers, sometimes to watch geese or ducks swimming, or to wave at a boat passing by. One day, we were within a few feet of a large moose.

The eastern side of the trail is a dense forest of lodgepole pine trees that climb up the slope of Shadow Mountain. These are very tall, thin trees. The summit of Shadow Mountain is 10,155 feet elevation.

Grand Lake is Colorado's largest and deepest natural lake. It forms a continuous body of water with Shadow Mountain Lake, which is a manmade lake. These two lakes are separated by a canal with gates. The Colorado River flows from its headwaters high in the Never Summer Range in the northwestern Colorado Rocky Mountains, down through western Rocky Mountain National Park, and into and through Shadow Mountain Lake. Shadow Mountain Dam is at the southern end of the lake. The Colorado River flows on south from the dam to Lake Granby. From there it continues on to help provide water to the southwestern United States. Water collected in Lake Granby is also pumped to Shadow Mountain and Grand Lake, then pumped under the Continental Divide through the Alva B. Adams Tunnel to the Big Thompson River on the eastern side of the Rocky Mountains. This water is to help supply parts of the eastern United States.

On our hike, when we reached Shadow Mountain Dam, we hiked across the top of the dam to Green Ridge Campground. From there we could watch boats being launched into the southern end of Shadow Mountain Lake. After a leisurely stroll around the campgrounds, we retraced our steps back across the dam, and followed the trail back along the lake, reaching our car a few hours later.

Another interesting feature worth noting on Shadow Mountain is the Shadow Mountain Overlook Tower. This was at one time a fire detection tower. We did not climb the several mile long, steep trail to the tower, but I have heard that once there, you can climb the stairs to the third level where there is an observation deck that wraps around the tower. The tower is at 9,923 feet elevation and the views from that deck are magnificent, including the lakes below, the Continental Divide, and the Never Summer Mountain Range.

One day, when my husband Bill was working, I drove up Trail Ridge Road alone, higher and higher, sometimes almost seeming to be a part of the clouds.

In summer and on weekends, often the road was covered with bumper to bumper traffic. And in winter, the higher regions of the road are closed, completely snow packed.

It must have been after Labor Day, after the summer traffic and before the snows came, that I made this trip. I passed other cars while driving on the road, but the parking lot overlooking a deep canyon was empty. I parked the car and started hiking down a steep path into the canyon. I never saw another soul on that hike. I walked down for a long time, surrounded by mountains. It is hard to describe how I felt, like a tiny speck in this vast quiet land of sky and mountains. I hiked down and further down to the bottom where the land leveled out somewhat. I walked on past tiny little lakes and through masses of wildflowers.

I was totally alone, and yet never have I so experienced the grandeur of God and of the universe. And the quietness...quieter than quiet. I longed to stay there indefinitely, but I knew I needed to turn around and start back up the mountain.

The memory and the feeling of that experience will stay with me forever.

During the year or so that we lived in Estes Park, I often drove in the mornings for about a half hour to places where I would hike for maybe an hour. There were three places in particular that I liked to hike.

One was south of Estes Park on Highway 7 which curved and climbed up a mountain side. When it leveled off at the top, there was a beautiful lake, Lily Lake, to the right of the road. Sometimes I just walked the path all the way around the lake. But other times, I climbed up a mountain path and hiked on a path across the top. This path bordered the northern edge of the lake and overlooked the lake. There was at least one bench where you could sit to admire the awesome view of Longs Peak (the only 14,000 footer in the Park). Enos Mills, the "Father of Rocky Mountain National Park", used to enjoy walking the one mile from his cabin, which was not far from the base of Long's Peak, to Lily Lake.

To get to the second place where I hiked, I drove west and into the southern entrance to Rocky Mountain National Park and on for 15 minutes or so to Deer Mountain. I loved to hike there. I started out climbing on the main path, but one lucky day I spotted a trail that led off the main trail. It went along the edge of that mountain, so I had watch my footing. But I often stopped to look at the incredible view to the south...Long's Peak, Flattop Mountain, Hallett Peak and others. A ranger told me that there are over 100 mountain peaks in the Park that are 11,000 feet or higher.

Only once do I recall meeting another person while hiking on that side trail. He was an elderly gentleman, a retired pastor from Minnesota. He told me that during all his years as a pastor in Minnesota, every summer he and his wife would drive a group of youngsters all the way from Minnesota to Estes Park to Rocky Mountain National Park. They loved the park and wanted the children to experience it. After he retired, they moved to Estes Park. He told me that he tried to hike every day, because when he didn't, he could feel it.

The trail eventually turned to the left through masses of wildflowers, and then connected back again to the main trail. Going down the mountain on that trail, I eventually reached my starting point. Sometimes I hiked more than once around that circle.

The third place where I liked to hike was along the long road that led from Horseshoe Park to Endovalley Park at the base of Old Fall River Road. One day I walked cautiously along the road because there were small herds of elk on either side of the road. It was near that road that I spotted the new tiny baby deer that I mentioned in the short story EXPLORE IT in the first IT Book. In the winter, that part of the road was closed to cars, but it was still open to hikers.

When I reached Endovalley Park, a small picnic area, the road went around in a circle. Along the southern edge of the park is beautiful, swiftly flowing Fall River. I loved to sit there and look and listen to that water. To the south of the river, high mountains rise to the sky.

Now we live far from Rocky Mountain National Park, but very often I relive our hikes there. To renew body and soul, at least in your mind

HIKE IT

EXPERIENCE IT

During the year after we moved from Evergreen, Colorado, to Estes Park, Colorado, I drove once a week to Evergreen to teach my piano students there for two days. Good friends let me stay overnight in their homes.

During the summer, in good weather, in daylight hours, I drove to Evergreen through the mountains on the Peak to Peak Highway, a Scenic Byway. It was a beautiful ride up majestic mountains, down into peaceful green valleys covered with wildflowers, around many curves, through several little towns, seeing few cars and very few people. It took about three hours.

I started south on Highway 7 out of Estes Park. I drove through Allenspark, home of the highly praised Meeker Park Lodge, founded and owned by the Dever family since 1922. At Raymond, I turned south onto Highway 72. I drove through Jamestown, Ward, and Nederland. Eldora Ski Resort is just a few minutes outside of Nederland. This is about 20 miles west of Boulder up the mountain. Highway 72 that continues south becomes Highway 119 through Rollinsville. I then drove further south down the mountain to Black Hawk. Before long I reached Interstate 70 just east of Idaho Springs. I drove a few miles east on I-70 to the Bergen Park exit and then down into Evergreen.

I often stayed overnight for two nights in Evergreen, but

one week I decided to drive back to Estes Park in the late afternoon. At that time of day, I did not make the drive back through the mountains. Instead I drove down the mountain on I-70 to the Golden exit, not far from Denver. From Golden, I started driving north on Highway 93. This is a well-travelled good highway that goes almost due north.

When driving down the mountain, it started to rain, and by the time I turned north on Highway 93, I found myself in a rainstorm with fierce winds.

Holding firmly onto the steering wheel, I kept driving slowly, trying to hold to the road. All at once, I heard the loudest noise of my life. The wild winds blowing down a mountain canyon to the left were carrying huge golf ball size hail that pounded my car. The windshield broke in about eight places, but thankfully didn't collapse inward because it was made of safety glass. The road looked like and was a sheet of ice. I pulled off to the side of the road, and put my hands over my ears to try to lessen the deafening noise. The lightning and wind and rain and hail seemed to last forever. I sat there praying my heart out, knowing that these could be the last minutes of my life if any of those huge balls of ice broke through my small car and hit me.

At last, except for the wind and rain, there was quietness. It was now pitch dark except for the terrific ongoing lightning displays. I tried to call my husband, Bill, in Estes Park on my cell phone, but couldn't make the connection because of the storm. He had no idea of my plight, as the weather was relatively calm in Estes Park.

It was so dark that I could only see the road when the lightning struck, and then only through one of the cracks in the shattered windshield. It was cold too. I couldn't just sit there, so I began slowly, cautiously driving. I still had to drive north for many miles, through Boulder, and all the way to the town of Lyons, where I would turn west and very carefully navigate up the steep mountain, around curves, and hope there would be no deer, elk or other wildlife on the road. After what should have been about a three hour drive, after what seemed like an eternity, I arrived safely home in Estes Park, sometime during the night.

EXPERIENCE IT

STUDY IT

In 1965, I graduated from Mundelein College, Chicago, with a B.A. in Music. In the late 1960s, I took several adult education classes in sewing.

I have spent much of my adult life taking postgraduate college courses. I love to learn.

In the 1970s, I drove to Central College in Pella, Iowa, for a couple years to take part-time courses in The Teaching of Reading. At the end of those courses, I did some student teaching at North High School in Des Moines, Iowa.

In the 1980s, I spent a year taking college courses in German.

In 1991, I studied Alphabetic Phonics at the Payne Education Center in Oklahoma City, Oklahoma. I earned six graduate hours of Multisensory Reading I from Oklahoma City University. This was Introductory Alphabetic Phonics Teacher Training.

I found Alphabetic Phonics to be extremely fascinating, practical and rewarding. Alphabetic Phonics teaches not only reading, but also handwriting, spelling, spoken and written communication, and comprehension.

I studied this and taught it to individuals with dyslexia. If I had not moved out of state, I think that with the instruction and support of the Payne Education Center, I could have enjoyed teaching Alphabetic Phonics for the rest of my life.

Stated very simply, in school most reading is taught utilizing the two methods of seeing (visual) and hearing (auditory). Dyslexics learn best utilizing a multisensory approach that includes seeing and hearing, but also utilizes kinesthetic learning, or learning by doing.

Dys is a Greek prefix meaning "hard".

Lexi is a Greek stem meaning "words".

Dyslexic means having a hard time learning and using the words of a language.

In one of our first classes, a neurosurgeon came and talked to us. He was interested in helping us because he had two dyslexic sons of his own who had been helped by Alphabetic Phonics.

He drew what he said was an extremely simplified picture of the brain in order to get a point across to us. On the left side of the board, he drew the left brain. On the right side of the board, he drew the right brain.

In the left brain, he drew a great many little circles, signifying cells.

In the right brain, he drew a lesser number of circles, cells.

He said that the majority of people have more cells in the left brain. The left brain is logical. It organizes thoughts and can communicate them by speaking in a logical sequence. It is skilled with numbers. Accountants are left brain individuals.

A smaller number of people have a greater number of cells in the right brain. Right brain individuals easily see things as images or pictures. A right brain individual likes to draw pictures when taking notes. People who learn best by doing are right brain. They often find letters on the page to be like "Greek" to them. They learn speech sounds by talking, speaking them. They learn cursive handwriting, for example, by drawing the letter in the air or on the blackboard, using the movement of their muscles.

Every activity of Alphabetic Phonics is designed to incorporate this right brain, kinesthetic type of learning, along with visual and auditory learning. It is, therefore, multisensory. In Alphabetic Phonics, a specially trained teacher or language therapist teaches the letters, one at a time, in a certain order, blending the name, the sound, the shape and the "feel" of each letter.

Many very famous people were dyslexic. Here are a few of them:

Thomas Edison – inventor

Leonardo da Vinci, Michaelangelo – sculptors, artists, painters

Tom Cruise, John Wayne, George Burns - actors

Walt Disney – film maker, animator

Fred Epstein – neurosurgeon

Bruce Jenner, Muhammed Ali, Magic Johnson – athletes

Charles Lindbergh, The Wright Brothers – pilots

Can you see how these are right brain people? Their great talents involve imagery and doing, such as artists, actors, pilots, inventors, singers, film makers, song writers, neurosurgeons, athletes.

The dyslexic individuals I taught had previously been taught only by the seeing/hearing methods, had failed to learn, and considered themselves failures.

When I taught them by the Alphabetic Phonics method, utilizing the kinesthetic or hands on approach, they succeeded in learning, and their joy knew no bounds.

They simply need to be taught the way their brains are programmed to learn.

STUDY IT

DRIVE IT

In the ten years that my husband, Bill, and I lived in the Colorado mountains, we loved to explore, not only by hiking, but also by driving.

Bill and I estimate that we drove between 30,000 and 40,000 miles sightseeing and exploring in Colorado during those ten years. This did not count miles for anything else.

About a third of those miles were spent driving to, from, and in Rocky Mountain National Park. During the many years that we lived in Evergreen, Colorado, we sometimes drove from Evergreen to Estes Park to reach the eastern entrances to Rocky Mountain National Park. But often, we drove from Evergreen to Grand Lake to reach the western entrance. This is an incredible trip. We drove west on I-70 to exit 232, then north on Highway 40 through Empire, and on up the mountain to Berthoud Pass at the Continental Divide, elevation 11,315 feet. This is a former ski area. In warm weather, we sometimes parked at the pass and hiked partway up to the summit.

We then continued our drive on Highway 40 down the winding mountainside north of Berthoud Pass to Winter Park, a well-known ski area and delightful town. The Winter Park Ski Area opened in 1939-1940. The summit elevation is 12,060 feet, and 9,000 feet at the base.

We then drove six miles north of Winter Park to Fraser.

Bill and I have always had a special feeling for Fraser. For one thing, there is a lovely little park called History Park at the Fraser Visitor Center. It was a good stopping place to relax and stretch our legs, to enjoy the mountain views. But the main reason that we have such a good feeling about Fraser is Doc Susie.

Dr. Susan Anderson (1870-1960) graduated from the University of Michigan Medical School in 1897. She was diagnosed with "a touch of T.B." while in medical school. A series of events led her, in December of 1907, to the little mountain town of Fraser, Colorado, to the drier, cold mountain air. Her tuberculosis had worsened, and she felt that this was her only hope of beating it. Later, she told someone: "I came here to die, but since I didn't get the job done, I guess I'll just have to live here instead."

She did live there for nearly 50 years until 1956. She dedicated her life as a doctor, to treating ranch families, and lumberjacks and their families in remote lumber camps. She was a little woman, with mighty determination and boundless courage.

We own and have read several times the book, *Doc Susie*, by Virginia Cornell, copyright 1991, about her life. We have seen the outside of the cabin in Fraser where she lived.

We then continued our drive to Granby where we turned right onto Highway 34. We drove past Lake Granby, Shadow Mountain Lake, and Grand Lake to the town of Grand Lake.

Grand Lake holds many happy memories for us. We have been there at every time of year. In summertime, we have walked the sandy beach at the lake, and sat on benches on the dock to watch the swimmers and the boats. We just relaxed and looked at the water and the awesome views in every direction. We have walked the streets of Grand Lake in every season. We have camped overnight there, and one time in the middle of the night, I saw a big bear overturn a heavy dumpster in a search for food, right in downtown Grand Lake.

We have spent memorable hours at Grand Lake Lodge, which was established in 1920. It is located high on a hill overlooking Grand Lake Village, Grand Lake, and Shadow Mountain Lake. The view from the long front porch of Grand Lake Lodge is breathtaking. I could sit there peacefully for hours, looking at the lakes, the boats, the mountains. The Lodge is bordered on three sides by Rocky Mountain National Park.

It is just a few minutes' drive from Grand Lake Lodge to the Kawuneeche Visitor Center and the western entrance to Rocky Mountain National Park. From there, one can drive the 39.9 miles up and across Trail Ridge Road, (that is a story in itself), and down to Estes Park, which is near the eastern entrances to the Park.

DRIVE IT

CREATE IT

The first book I wrote was *Beginning Piano: The Way I Teach It.*

This book evolved from 25 years of teaching piano.

Is there anything more inspirational in the world than truly beautiful music?

I was extremely blessed to be raised in a musical family. My grandmother, Agnes Antoinette Flynn, to whom I dedicated my book, was in the words of my mother "a concert pianist and organist." She did not travel the world and perform concerts, although she could have. Instead, she performed in her home for those close to her, and in church for the glory of God.

At age 15 she had completed a degree in music and was organist at St. Ambrose Cathedral in downtown Des Moines, Iowa. Years later in 1920, when she had been married for several years, her husband, my grandfather, Francis Patrick Flynn, and eleven other men petitioned Bishop T.W. Drumm and paid the necessary money to establish a parish on the west side of Des Moines. St. Augustin Church was formally dedicated in February 1924. My grandmother, at the request of Father John Noonan, the first pastor, became the first and only full-time organist for nearly 40 years, from the 1920s until a short time before her death in 1961. My father, Joseph

John Gedden, was the choir director and part-time organist for 35 years, from 1939 until his retirement in 1974.

I studied piano with Sister Mary Annunciata, B.V.M., at St. Joseph Academy from sixth through twelfth grades. I then earned a B.A. in Music, which included piano, at Mundelein College, Chicago.

My family did a great deal of singing, too, both at home and at church. So my life was truly filled with music.

I tell about my piano teaching career in the first *IT Book*, in the short story CHOOSE IT. I don't know at just what point I started to teach beginning piano using the method that I describe in *Beginning Piano: The Way I Teach It*. This method is based on PICTURING or VISUALIZING. Of course, the basics of the keys on the keyboard and the notes on the page are always the same, but the concept of picturing used at the beginning of every piano lesson, week after week, month after month (and practiced by the student day after day), is highly effective.

Many discouraged or only partially successful pianists never thoroughly learned the notes in the first place. Imagine trying to read if you had never really learned the alphabet. Thoroughly learning the keys on the keyboard and the notes on the page is as essential to learning to play the piano successfully as building a firm foundation is to having a sturdy, long lasting house.

This book can be successfully used by teachers of

beginning piano, or by any individual who can read and comprehend it and who earnestly wants to give him or herself a head start in learning to play the piano.

To develop a new way to teach age old concepts

CREATE IT

GO FOR IT

In an older version of Dale Carnegie's book, *How to Win Friends and Influence People*, I recently read something that has changed my life. It was actually a sentence he had quoted. It was the motto of the King's Guard in ancient Greece. Here is the quote:

"All men have fears,

but the brave put down their fears and go forward,

sometimes to death,

but always to victory."

"All men have fears,

but the brave put down their fears and go forward."

In my life, I have experienced the full gamut in regard to fear. In my twenties and early thirties, I was possessed by fear, so much so that I underwent three separate months of shock treatments, three each week. The only "purpose" they served was to make me much more fearful, especially when, as often happened, I would wake up after a treatment and no one would be there, and I didn't know where I was.

During that time, I read: "There is nothing to fear but fear itself." That almost paralyzed me with fear because I knew I was afraid of fear. I had frequent panic attacks. The psychiatrist, who had worked with me for five years, gotten

34

me on drugs, and ordered all the shock treatments, gave up on me and refused to see or talk to me again. I began thinking of suicide.

The good part about all of that is that I began my desperate search for truth, for peace. This was a long search of many years, but I firmly believe, I don't just believe, I know, that if anyone will turn to God and pray, and never give up, God will answer. He may not answer in just the way we want, but He will answer in the way that is best for us. He sees the whole picture. We see only a tiny part.

We are, every single one of us, God's children, created and loved by Him. If sometimes His answers seem painfully slow, it is not because He is slow. Rather (and it is good to have a sense of humor about this), it is because He has to find ways to work around all of our fears, strange ideas, and habits. He finds ways that we can tolerate, that won't overwhelm us.

I firmly believe that what I heard my mother say over and over the last year of her life, "Keep on keeping on", is one of the main keys to leading a successful life, successful in the eyes of God, that is.

Another book by Dale Carnegie, *How to Stop Worrying and Start Living*, has and is helping me more than words can tell. The irony of it is that I had this book in a plastic binder, along with cassette tapes of the entire book, for maybe 20 years or more. I bought it on a terrific sale, and then never touched the book. It was still brand new when one day I got the idea that some friends of mine might be helped by it. I sent them the tapes and kept the book. I began to read the book to see how my friends could be helped by the tapes. See what I mean about having a sense of humor and about the infinite patience God has in dealing with us? Of course, the book was the very thing that I myself needed!

I have read and reread and underlined and marked with bookmarks the pages that help me the most.

On the first page of the first chapter, Dale Carnegie tells that a worried young medical student read a quote that enabled him to live a life free from worry. Freed from worry, which saps our life energy, he went on to become the most famous physician of his generation and founder of the world-famous Johns Hopkins School of Medicine. His name was Sir William Osler.

Here is the quote that freed him from worry, a quote by Thomas Carlyle: "Our main business is not to see what lies dimly at a distance, but to do what lies clearly at hand."

"TO DO WHAT LIES CLEARLY AT HAND"

I have never had such peace and such joy as I have since I started living this way.

Whenever I start on my old path of worry and fear or of "eternally" rehashing the past, I just pull myself to the present and "do what lies clearly at hand." It is so energizing. It brings such joy and accomplishment, such freedom. Since I started living this way, I have published three books, and this will be the fourth.

Years later, Sir William Osler, in an address to the students of Yale University, urged them to live in "day-tight compartments", not in the past, not in the future, but today. He told them:

"The load of tomorrow, added to that of yesterday, carried today, makes the strongest falter."

He also urged the Yale students to begin the day with Christ's prayer: "Give us this day our daily bread." It really struck me when Dale Carnegie wrote: "Today's bread is the only kind of bread you can possibly eat."

It has been over 40 years since I had those shock treatments. I have gone from being possessed by fear to having such peace as I never dreamed possible.

Pray, love the God who made you, who knows and loves you, be patient with yourself, and, as Sir Winston Churchill said:

"Never, never, never, never give up."

I once read that this life on earth "is a schoolroom, not a playground."

We can learn to become still enough inside to hear the voice of God speaking to us, each one, maybe not often in so many words, but in silent nudges in the right direction, the direction that if persistently followed will lead us to peace, to Him.

"Be still and know that I AM God." Psalm 46:10

We don't have to be sick or to suffer to learn life's lessons, but it seems that many of us do. I know that I would never have made all the changes I needed to make if I hadn't experienced what I did.

And when at times you fail, hear these comforting words that I have so often heard:

"Arise, my child, and try again, and keep on trying."

GO FOR IT

ACCEPT IT

We human beings seem to have the hardest time accepting things, from the smallest interruptions in our day to the death of those we love. Somehow we would like to get our lives in perfect order and keep them that way forever. We would like to keep ourselves and all in our lives safe and free from pain or hurt of any kind.

Yet life is constant change, forever challenging us, molding us.

When I was in high school, the mother of a friend of mine often said the serenity prayer.

"God, grant me the serenity

to accept the things I cannot change,

the courage to change the things I can,

and the wisdom to know the difference."

Through the years, I have often puzzled over the meaning of those words.

All of my adult life, I have fought to stay alive, to heal. From my early thirties, I have been unable to process the food I ate. I became increasingly sensitive to foods.

For years, I sought answers in the medical field. I became addicted to pharmaceutical drugs, and finally, in an agonizing month in the early eighties, I wrenched myself off of them.

I have tried countless paths in alternative medicine, but

every time that I finished some program of healing, right when I should have experienced health, there was always a "brick wall" that I found myself up against. I kept trying for the past 40 years, one thing after another, always running into that brick wall. I have often thought that if anyone tried as hard as I had to heal, they would be so healthy they wouldn't know what to do with themselves.

The foods that I ate moved so slowly through my digestive system that they hardly moved at all, causing of course, multiple diseases.

I studied the healing properties of foods. I exercised. I tried juice diets, detoxifying diets. You name it. But I was constantly getting sick when I ate most foods.

My immune system kept getting weaker and weaker, and I became allergic to chemicals. It became harder for me to teach because I couldn't be around perfume, cologne, hair spray, scented candles, and many other chemicals.

I always wondered why I never seemed to be able to build muscles in my arms and legs, even though I walked and exercised. I wondered why I couldn't kick my legs when I tried to swim.

I fiercely fought to get well. I believed that I would. I tried with all my heart. I prayed with all my heart. I have driven doctors and healers of all kinds to their limits in my search for answers.

A couple years ago, I lost 25 pounds that I didn't need to

lose. I weighed 100. I had to stop teaching. Then I had to stop driving because, after several close calls, I knew that my reflexes were too slow to drive safely. I have become weaker and sometimes think that I am living in another world from my neighbors and friends. This past year I lost 20 more pounds. I now weigh 80 and my body can tolerate only two foods and those in liquid form.

Why am I writing this? Why am I sharing all of this that I have so carefully guarded during all of my life of nearly 74 years?

I always thought that to accept my condition would be to give up, to be a quitter.

I have come to believe that we don't always get things just the way we pray for them, just the way we want them to be, even good things like health. I have come to realize that there are other kinds of healing more important than physical healing, such as healing of the mind, healing of emotions, the healing that brings peace even in the midst of physical distress and pain.

A few years ago, I learned the cause of all those "brick walls" I ran into in all my attempts to heal. It is a progressive form of paralysis that affects the muscles of my arms and legs and the nerves of my bowel. Knowing this has answered nearly all the questions I have had about my digestive system, my weakened immune system, and my health in general. It has given me great peace of mind.

I just now realized the meaning of the first line of that Serenity Prayer.

"God, grant me the serenity to accept the things I cannot change."

Until now, I have always dwelt on the part "to accept the things I cannot change", and I rebelled against that. When I reread it a moment ago, I saw "God, grant me the serenity". In seeing that I had the correct diagnosis, God gave me serenity. He granted me the serenity that I needed to accept the things I cannot change.

At last, I have been able to

ACCEPT IT

UPLIFT IT

I love mountains. Is there anything more uplifting than a mountain?

When my husband, Bill Mercer, and I lived in Evergreen, Colorado, we knew of a husband and wife who were planning to move to the San Juan mountains in southwest Colorado. One day in a store, I heard someone ask the woman why they would want to move there. I will never forget her answer.

"Have you SEEN the San Juans?" she asked.

Fourteen of Colorado's fifty-three 14,000 foot mountains are in the San Juans. The highest point is Uncompahgre Peak at 14,309 feet elevation. The San Juan mountains cover over 12,000 square miles. They are extremely steep, and for that reason, Telluride is the only major ski resort. There are two other smaller ones, however. Durango Mountain Resort (formerly Purgatory) is just 25 miles north of Durango on U.S. Highway 550. Wolf Creek Ski area is 26 miles east of Pagosa Springs on U.S. Highway 160.

The San Juans have been called "Shining Mountains" by the Ute Indians. They have also been called "God's Country". Some think that the San Juans are the most beautiful mountains in the world.

Bill and I have driven to the San Juans five times. Twice, we made the 700 mile round trip from Evergreen to the San Juans and then on to Mesa Verde National Park (which is another story in itself). Since we have lived in Albuquerque, New Mexico, we have driven north into the San Juans, and also to Mesa Verde, three times.

On U. S. Highway 550, we drove from Albuquerque to Durango. From Durango, we followed 550 north up, up, and higher up into the beautiful San Juans to the town of Silverton.

The Durango and Silverton Narrow Gauge Railroad is a coal-burning, steam-powered locomotive that travels the same tracks that cowboys, miners, and settlers followed over a hundred years ago. Travelers can take this trip in summer months through the awesome canyons in San Juan National Forest.

In Silverton, we walked the short hike up to Christ of the Mines monument on Anvil Mountain which overlooks the town. This is a 16 foot tall statue of Jesus. It was carved by hand from Carrara marble in Italy. It weighs 12 tons. It was shipped from Italy in several pieces and was put together in Silverton.

Silverton is connected to Ouray by the 25 mile long Million Dollar Highway. The Million Dollar Highway is also U.S. Highway 550 and is part of the San Juan Scenic Skyway. It goes over Red Mountain Pass at 11,018 feet elevation. We stopped at that pass, walked to overlooks to see the incredible views, and enjoyed the wildflowers.

Red Mountain Pass summit is the county line between

Ouray and San Juan counties.

We then started driving down the northern side of Red Mountain Pass. What I remember most and will never forget were the portions of the highway that went around tight curves and that overlooked Uncompahgre Gorge that is so deep you can hardly see the bottom, that is, if you are brave enough to look down. And there were NO GUARDRAILS! Bill did the driving there. However, we were greatly rewarded when the road wound around and down into the town of Ouray, the Switzerland of America.

Ouray is hard to describe in words. In the masterful photography book, Spirit of the SAN JUANS by Kathleen Norris Cook, one can see on pages 48 and 49 a picture of Ouray as we saw it with our own eyes. The book measures 12 inches by almost 12 inches, so the pictures are not small.

Ouray is nestled at the base of and surrounded by very steep 12,000 to 13,000 foot mountains. Ouray itself is about 7,800 feet in elevation.

We drove in and around the small town. We stopped at The Ouray Hot Springs Pool which was built in 1927. We parked the car in downtown Ouray and walked up and down Main Street which is a National Historic District. Most of the buildings were built in the late 1800s and have been restored to their original beauty. Then we walked east on Eighth Avenue one fourth mile to the base of Cascade Falls, one of the loveliest waterfalls that we have ever seen. The falls can be seen from many places in the town.

Next we drove the eleven miles north to Ridgway, Colorado. Ridgway is "the Gateway to the San Juans" from the north. It was established in 1891 and is 6,985 feet in elevation. It is surrounded by majestic mountains.

John Wayne's movies, "True Grit" and "How the West Was Won" were filmed there. The Rio Grande Southern railroad was centered in Ridgway and serviced the mining towns of Ouray and Telluride. Bald eagles are commonly seen in Ridgway in the fall. They nest in cottonwoods along the Uncompahgre River.

Ridgway is the northern entrance to the San Juan Skyway, a highway of 233 miles which offers some of the most beautiful views in the San Juans. Bill and I have travelled almost every area of the San Juan Skyway.

The following is the most direct route from Ridgway to Telluride.

Go west out of Ridgway on CO Highway 62. Turn left on CO Highway 145. There is a sign showing a left turn to Telluride. Follow CO-145 for about 16 miles straight into Telluride.

However, we learned from someone in Ridgway that we could travel west on CO-62 and look for Last Dollar Road. The turnoff to the left is about 12 miles west of Ridgway. The road is about 18 miles long. It is a dirt jeep road, at least it when we were there. For fun, we took this road to Telluride.

At the time we were there, we hardly saw another car or another person on that road. We did, however, see inspiring mountain views and a huge flock of sheep. The road ended on CO-145 near the Telluride Airport.

In 1878 the town of Columbia was established. In 1887 the town was renamed Telluride. Telluride is a former silver mining camp on the San Miguel River. The Telluride Historic District is one of Colorado's 20 National Historic Landmarks.

Black Bear Road, a dirt road, winds up the mountain at the east end of Telluride. Ingram Falls to the north and Bridal Veil Falls to the south are also at the eastern end high above Telluride. Bridal Veil Falls is 365 feet high, the tallest falls in Colorado.

In 1972, Telluride Ski Resort was opened and then developed by Joseph Zoline of Beverly Hills, California.

The town of Telluride is surrounded by some of the most beautiful scenery on earth.

We then drove down The San Juan Skyway, on CO-145, from Telluride to Cortez on U.S. Highway 160, a distance of 76 miles. The entrance to Mesa Verde National Park is ten miles east of Cortez on Highway 160. It is about a 50 mile drive further east on Highway 160 to Durango, our Colorado starting point into the beautiful San Juans.

"I will lift up my eyes to the hills.
From whence comes my help?
My help comes from the Lord,
Who made heaven and earth."
Psalm 121

UPLIFT IT

FINISH IT

"There is a time to be born
and a time to die."
Ecclesiastes 3:2

It may seem rather strange for an author to talk about his or her own death, but that is what I seem led to do, perhaps to help alleviate some of the fear that is associated with death.

As a child, I was full of questions about life and death. How in the world could a God who is my Father create a hell? This made zero sense to me. What good earthly father would do that to his child, let alone a God who is perfect?

How could God who is perfect create something that is imperfect, especially something horrid, like hell? Impossible!

I have come to know that hell is not a place. Hell is what we experience within ourselves when we turn away from God, when we do not follow His promptings within us, our conscience, when we are not loving and kind to Him, to ourselves and to each other.

God gave us free will or free choice so we could freely choose to love Him. Love cannot be forced. God is all about Love. We can turn back to Him at any moment day or night, as the Prodigal Son did in the Bible, and be welcomed home and forgiven. But in God's eyes, as in the eyes of the father of the Prodigal Son, we are and always have been His children.

To me, hell was the fear I lived in earlier in my life. Now as I draw nearer to my own death, heaven is a continuance of the peace that passes understanding, the peace that I am so very gratefully experiencing now.

To pass on to the next life without fear, with peace, even with great joy, we need to make our peace with God and man. We need to resolve or to ask God to help us resolve anything that we know is keeping us from being peaceful. If we are peaceful when we leave here, we can be sure we will be peaceful in the life to come, because that peace is within ourselves.

My beloved father, Joseph John Gedden, about whom I wrote my book *My Father*, told me that at the time he had a cerebral aneurysm, he went through a Tunnel of Light that was so beautiful it was indescribable. He said that he was given a choice to go on into that Light or to come back. He so wanted to go on, but he chose to come back to take care of his new baby son, his wife, and the rest of his family.

He told me years later as he neared the end of his life on earth: "All doors are secondary to that door", the door into that Light that he had experienced years before. He died as he had lived, in peace.

FINISH IT

POEMS

FROM MY HEART

A WORLD OF KINDNESS

Is there anything in the world more important than
kindness?

It is a smile, a gentle word, an understanding heart,
patient thoughtfulness, a caring heart, taking time to listen to
our hearts and follow our inner guidance, loving God and
loving our neighbor as ourselves.

What would happen to our world if everyone was kind,
all the time?
There would be no more wars, no crime, no jails, no
prisons, no greed, no power struggles, no hunger, no want,
no poverty, no homelessness, no fear.

There would be good will, communication,
understanding, sharing solutions for the good of each and all,
peace, prosperity, gratitude and joy.

A World of Kindness
It would be "on earth as it is in Heaven".

SOWING AND REAPING

Life is a circle.
What we sow, we reap,
in our lives as in our gardens.

Every word, every thought,
every feeling, every action
goes forth in a circle,
collecting more of its kind,
and returns to us one day,
the good and the lesser.

This is the responsibility
of free will, the gift of
God that enables us to love.

PEACE

That quiet place
that nothing can disturb

The goal of every
human striving

The greatest comfort
one can find

Peace of heart and
soul and mind.

JOY

Joy cometh in the morning
to a peaceful heart.

Joy cometh in the evening
after a day well lived.

Joy cometh in unexpected hours,
a treasured gift.

Joy dwells within
a grateful heart.

Joy abides in the universe
singing its song of praise
to the heart of creation.

For joy
we are so very thankful.

HUMMINGBIRDS

Tiny joy givers, entertainers,
fun!

Darting, diving, daring,
flying up and down
to and fro.

Cruising, pausing, playing,
eating, staring inside our
window, staring into
my eyes.

Zooming to the tiptop of
a high tree beyond the back wall,
and in a flash appearing on
the bird feeder next to the house.

Fearless little flyers.
We love you.

A ROSE

What is so lovely
as a rose?
Subject of how
many poems?

Delicate, gentle,
colorful, beguiling,
fragrant, exquisite

Simply by being.

COLORING

Relaxing, challenging,

Choosing, mixing,
blending, enjoying
colors.

Learning, growing,
shading, observing,
pondering, conferring
with Bill.

Accomplishing,
however simple,
a thing of beauty.

RAIN

Refreshing, renewing,
replenishing rain.

Joy of grass and trees
and birds and flowers,
of all living things.

Joyful, peaceful,
restful,
the sound of rain.

Life taking care
of its own.

MRS. DOVE

Outside our window in a tree
patiently sitting on your eggs.
How long have you been there?
Faithful through wind and
heat and storm, through
seemingly endless nights
and days that stretch
into weeks.

Example of motherhood,
selfless and loving,
faithfully expecting,
nurturing,
believing

in the miracle of life.

THIS MAY

The most beautiful Spring
cool but not cold
lovely rain showers often
trees so grateful for the rain
happy birds singing
hummingbirds darting to and fro.

Roses blooming in many colors
two huge bunches of miniature pink carnations
snapdragons towering over them
little marigolds
adding their touch of color.

Thank you, God, for May.
Thank you, God, for Spring.
Thank you, God, for everything.

FRIENDSHIP

Giving and receiving
Loving and caring
Listening and understanding
Laughing and crying
Praying and uplifting
Sharing and growing.

Love is what sustains us.

A true friend is
the music of life
for time and eternity.

UNLESS YOU BECOME AS LITTLE CHILDREN

Nobuyuki Tsujii, Van Cliburn,
Horowitz, Rubenstein,
and my Nana.

Childlike, humble,
kind, caring, grateful
as little children.

His children
through whom He
can express
His greatest beauty.

Ambassadors of Peace
through whom He
can express
His Healing.

CHOPIN

Nobu, Rubenstein,
Van Cliburn
Horowitz
and my Nana.

Lovers of Chopin,
expressing the
beauty and
healing of God
through the music
of Chopin.

Vessels of beauty
Thank you!

GIVING

God has an
eternal need
to GIVE.

Giving is His
delight.

Giving of His
Life, His Light, His Love,
His Joy, His All.

And we are
His Children.

ANGELS

Angels ever at our side
Angels for our every need
Angels full of Love and Light

Angels – giving is
their delight.

Angels to protect
and to guard

Angels, God's Messengers
great and small.

Angels waiting
for our call.

LIFE'S JOURNEY

Ups and downs
Hills and valleys
Highs and lows
Calm and storms
Joys and sorrows
Peace and pain

Success and failure
Reunions and partings
Questions and answers

Through it all we learn.
Through it all
He guides us Home.

TO EVERYTHING A SEASON

The ebb and flow
of the tide

Sunrise and sunset

Winter, spring,
summer, fall

Planting, growing,
harvest

Our inbreath
and our outbreath

Night and day

A time to be born
and a time to die

To everything a season.

SPRING

Flowers blooming
heralding spring

Trees leafing
miracle of renewal

Seeds coming alive
in the ground

Blossoms on fruit trees
preparing to bear fruit

Birds singing
happy songs

Sleeping hearts uplifted
with hope

All life rising
as Christ
from the dead.

HOME

Water flowing
flowing home

Birds rising
flying home

Mountains reaching
reaching for home

All life seeking
seeking Home

Made in the USA
Charleston, SC
08 June 2016